Sacred Connections

Jaina Keshav Patel

BookLeaf Publishing

Presentation by *BookLeaf Publishing*

Web: www.bookleafpub.com

E-mail: info@bookleafpub.com

ISBN: 9789357615198

First edition 2022

If all the world were flowers –

I'd pick you.

Again.

ACKNOWLEDGEMENT

I have to start by thanking my friends. Halima and Kellie who read my early work and encouraged me to be my authentic self. Sofia and Priya, thank you so much for helping me edit and pushing me to believe that my poems could live past a plasma screen. I'm grateful to the team at BookLeaf Publications - special mention to Arushi and Muskaan for their valuable support and kindness. All of you made this dream a reality.

My Parents, my sister Maya and anyone who has ever said anything positive to me or has given me guidance – I listened and learnt. Thank you.

PREFACE

As an only child for a long time, storytelling through songs was my favourite pastime. My only friends back then were the flowers in the gardens I spent time in. My first teachers were the elements and the environment – it was only fitting to include them all in this book.

Sathya

For without that I'd have never loved
and known what love could be.
Without which I cannot live in peace
amongst society.
Feeling bliss in all I do especially when
duty-bound,
loving those who have the most and especially
those without.

Sathya – Truth

Tolerance

I see you all day,
and trust you all night,
and still watch as we all consume you.

I stopped and stalled,
Ignored, ignored
and ignored the consequences of
our treatment of you.

If the wind stopped blowing,
the rain stopped falling,
the sun stopped shining
and the earth stopped forgiving
Where would we all go?

Whilst the wind is blowing,
and the rain is falling
and the sun is shining
the earth continues to show

that…

the gentle wind has no ego,
showering rain discriminates never,
the blazing sun is punctual and
our earth provides forever.

Our selfless earth

The sun never says you owe me – for lighting up
your home.
The sea never asks for payment – for nourishing
your growth.
The earth never requests compensation – for
damaging her roots.
A life without reimbursement is her one simple
truth.

Without one it would be challenging to live
without the knowledge.
Without one it would be difficult to harvest any
food.
Without one it would be tough, since we can't
live without our homes.
Our lives would be less problematic –
if we saw them
as our own.

Faith

Living in trees is where I find peace, tuning into
the wisdom of nature.
Finding the time to quieten my mind – in spaces
created for adventure.

Bearing the weight of mountains, you carry the
never-ending sea.
In all the places you've created – you've carved
out a space for me.

Clutching my hand when I hold you,
having faith in the one I don't see.
Comforted in the conviction –
that in you I find
clarity.

A Mother's Promise

Bearing the burden of huge mountains,
drowning in the depths of the sea.
Accepting all the pain when we plough into her
–
she still provides food for me.

The road ahead was paved upon her,
towering buildings built to provide shelter.
Forbearing my trespasses when I walk over her
leading me to the places I dream.

Playgrounds filled with children,
where trees and hedges surround.
All nourished by the blazing sun and the
gentle breeze throughout.

She continues to give,
as we continue to want
her skin, her heart, her strength.

A mother's promise
to her children
kept.

An ode to the lonesome Wind

You carry out your mighty work, without us
even knowing.
Filling spaces with fresh air with pure love
overflowing.

Whispering sweet promises and sharing precious
truths.
You whisk away my cares and lighten my hectic
schedule.

Rustling leaves and swaying branches remind
me of your presence.
Seasons change, you remain the same -
a fountain of divine affection.

Rain falls

Rain falls generously, hydrating a farmer's thirst.
Nurturing life in steady waters, hungry prey
disturbed.

Water spreads selflessly, sweeping swiftly
through what surrounds it.
Flowing through pathways high and low, no
journey shapes it, no response is a 'No'
Humbly it fits – through gaps we see and even
those we don't.

Showers trickle cautiously, washing away sights
that brought fear.
Distant moments become a mystery; old pages
are now crystal clear.

Rain blesses generously, sharing love through
the songs it sings.
Washing away tears from yesterday, allowing
new chapters to begin.

Agni

Agni[1] burns bright and strong
dispelling darkness and
correcting wrong thoughts.
Spreading light.

Agni grows up and right,
our thoughts should follow,
stand up high.
Be kind, be nice.

Flames fly, sparks burn holes,
courageous thoughts shot into the unknown.
Energy shared.

Agni[1] – Fire

Suraj

Brightens the day without causing a blister.
Dispelling darkness and exposing the truth.
Providing light to those who otherwise may falter.
Heating lives of the destitute.

Giving without receiving.
Always turning up on time.
Never telling the Earth, "You owe me!"
for the light that it provides.

Selfless by nature, dependable by rule
Suraj[1] kabhi nahi doobta[2]
until it completes
what it lives to do.

Suraj[1] – Sun
kabhi nahi doobta[2] – never sets

Keshav

If the world was my back garden, you'd be the
sun that shone
constantly with love and light without which I'd
never have
begun.

If all the world was water, you'd be the
knowledge-filled bubbles that immersed
with me on my life journey, guiding me through
the sea of
love.

You are the wind I needed, to lift my wings
beyond,
to reach the goals I've succeeded in, whilst
staying humble
all along.

The fire in my belly, to achieve the things I've
wished,
started when you showed me
a life that is enriched.

Kusum

A foundation of security you created for us,
to steady the ship whenever we felt lost.
Gliding along the winds of right conduct,
following the direction of honesty and love.

An institute of values is what we came home to.
Wavering minds in life's stormy seas
search for you
still.

Clouds of doubt shift when we practice patience,
observing the education
that we hold
sacred.

Maya

Much listening is required,
to absorb the wisdom you share.

Always from God's lips to my ears,
is knowledge you declare.

You love me unconditionally –
give to all without hesitation.

A world made better by the presence of you.
Softened with – your thoughtful intentions.

Maa

My mother's prayers have always
saved me.
When I'm alone, I use the tools she gave me.
Shraddha[1] shakti[4]
Sahan[2] shakti
Samaj[3] shakti
are three
instruments I pray for and practice.
On life's generous journey.

Shraddha[1] – Faith
Shakti[2] – Strength
Sahan[3] – Tolerate/Endure
Samaj[4] – Understanding

The Truth about Kindness

Souls that cross by chance
and help without hesitation.
Expecting nothing.

Mine

Connections I have many,
through blood they weren't assigned.

From Birmingham to Middlesborough,
my family was devised.

Yoga trips in Newbury to keep us young and
limber.
Hours of tequila and talks near rivers
remembered.

If London was much closer, I'd see you more I
hope.
Over 20 years of travelling have kept our
friendship afloat.

Cycling is where we started, on road and
mountain bikes.
You're now a wonderful mother, yet still make
time for hikes.

The world's a large place but I'm lucky
to have a family chosen by me.
Sacred connections reflecting my values
keep me in
good company.

Other people

Other's weddings
Other's flowers
Other's hen do's
And other's baby showers.

We organise them, host them and make them entertaining.
2 am phone calls and late-night shopping when it's raining.

Floristry and therapy often work together.
Sushi, chips and pizza over conversations
that last
forever.

Child | less

"When you have children,
you'll understand the love
that you are missing…"
I hesitate to contradict,
due to the love I feel this instant.

My classroom

It's crowded but still lonely
when you walk in and you see me,
you feel at home.

The weight of your emotions,
weigh heavily upon me.
My words I watch carefully,
to make sure I cause no pain.

When rules are broken by you,
I don't scream and shout.
I don't tell you that you're senseless.
Instead, I try removing doubts, by reminding
you of
your worth.

Stranger

To the stranger on the street who walked me
home.
Carrying my furniture, up Ealing Road.
I'm grateful.

You left me at the high street, believing that I
lived there.
I hid behind the bus stop – so you wouldn't stop
and stare.
I didn't want you to know that I still had a mile.
To carry my furniture home.

I paused on the High Street and took a moment
to recover
and think about the road ahead.
That I hadn't really considered.

But… I've been here before and beaten the urge,
to shed tears over situations that accidentally
occur.

Wrapping my arms around the package, I held it
close and tight,
weaving my fingers through the torn handles, I
managed to get a grip.
Hold on, I whispered and prayed.

Within seconds a student started walking beside me.
He asked if I needed a hand.
I said I was fine, that I live up the road,
he grabbed a strap and said, 'me too, let's go home'.

We laughed and joked as we stumbled on the concrete.
Sharing our stories as we walked up the high street.
I swallowed my tears whilst he made me feel comfortable.
Accepting help from a stranger is painfully difficult.

Gifted literature

When mother Kaikeyi was misguided, she
inevitably taught me
the importance of keeping good company.
The behaviour of her offspring when they
refused her offerings
demonstrated an absent ego and potency.

A pillar of strength when all seemed lost,
Sitamaa didn't waver from her faith.
Hanumanji inspired me to be the friend
I yearn to be
a protector and loyal mate.

The troubles of Lord Rama taught me that life
can be uncertain,
obstacles will come and go
but all is necessary on this journey of life.
To develop our spiritual goals.

untitled

To all the people I didn't know,
who gifted me their time.
Thank you.
Those were the loneliest days
I survived.